BODYSCOPE

Life
Cycle

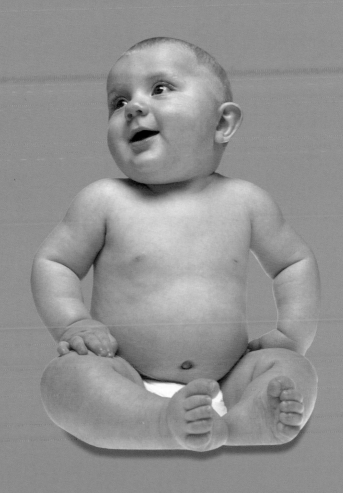

BODYSCOPE

Life Cycle

Birth, growth, and development

Dr. Patricia Macnair

Consultant:

Richard Walker

KINGFISHER

BOSTON

KINGFISHER

a Houghton Mifflin Company imprint
222 Berkeley Street
Boston, Massachusetts 02116
www.houghtonmifflinbooks.com

First published in 2004
10 9 8 7 6 5 4 3 2 1
1TR/0704/PROSP/PICA(PICA)/140MA/F

ISBN 0-7534-5780-6

Copyright © Kingfisher Publications Plc 2004

Author: Dr. Patricia Macnair
Consultant: Richard Walker
Editor: Clive Wilson
Coordinating editor: Caitlin Doyle
Designer: Peter Clayman
Illustrators: Sebastian Quigley, Guy Smith
Picture researcher: Kate Miller
Production controller: Lindsey Scott
DTP coordinator: Jonathan Pledge
DTP operator: Primrose Burton
Indexer: Sue Lightfoot

Contents

All in a lifetime

Just like every other person on the planet, you will go through many changes during your lifetime. These changes are part of the human life cycle, which begins with birth and ends with death. A new baby marks the beginning of a new life cycle.

▲ Every person develops from a tiny human egg like this one, seen under a microscope. Each egg is smaller than the period at the end of this sentence.

▼ This baby girl is welcomed by her family. When she grows up, she may have children of her own.

The circle of life

In order to create a new generation of children, men and women reproduce. Around the world more than 14,000 babies are born every hour—or four every second! Most will survive into adulthood and become parents themselves.

▲ This baby zebra is up and walking around soon after being born. It can look after itself without its mother's help.

Info lab

- Jeanne Calmet, from France, lived longer than any other person. She died in 1997 at the age of 122.

- Children under the age of 15 make up almost one-third of the people on our planet.

- Every minute the world's population increases by 140 people.

Raising a baby

Unlike many baby animals, human babies are completely helpless when they are born. It takes many years—first as a child and then as teenager—to learn the skills that you will need as an adult. During this time your parents take care of you, providing support and love.

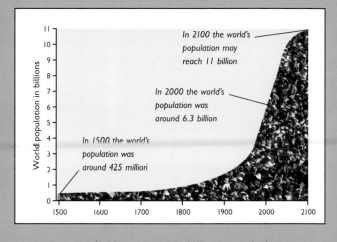

In 2100 the world's population may reach 11 billion

In 2000 the world's population was around 6.3 billion

In 1500 the world's population was around 425 million

World population in billions

▲ More than six billion people live on our planet. By 2100 there may be 11 billion.

Child of our time

One hundred years ago many children did not live past their fifth birthday. Today, with cleaner water and better health care, most children reach adulthood. In a developed country, such as the U.S., a baby girl born today can expect to live for 80 years.

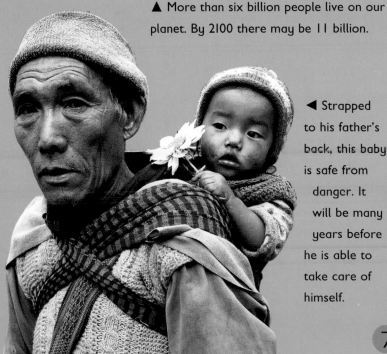

◀ Strapped to his father's back, this baby is safe from danger. It will be many years before he is able to take care of himself.

The male reproductive system

In order to reproduce, a man must make special cells, called sperm, and pass these on to a woman, to join with one of her eggs. To do this, a man has several reproductive organs. They include the testes, where sperm are made, the penis, and the prostate gland.

Sperm factories

Every day around 300 million new sperm are produced inside a man's testes—a pair of oval-shaped organs. Before the sperm leave the body they are mixed with fluids from the prostate gland. This provides them with fuel for the journey to the woman's egg.

Staying cool

Sperm need to be kept cool—at around 93°F (34°C). This is 37°F (3°C) below the temperature inside the body. To keep this temperature, the testes hang outside the body, where it is cooler, inside a pouch of skin called the scrotum.

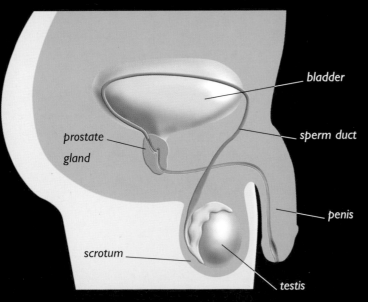

prostate gland

scrotum

bladder

sperm duct

penis

testis

◀ Sperm travel from the testes, along the sperm duct, and out through the penis. The reproductive system does not become fully developed until the teenage years.

▼ This microscopic picture of sperm shows their whiplike tails. The sperm use these to swim toward the woman's egg.

Being a man

The male reproductive system is controlled by chemical messengers, or hormones. One of these hormones—testosterone—makes men look different from women. It causes the voice to deepen, muscles to develop, and thick hair to grow on the face and body.

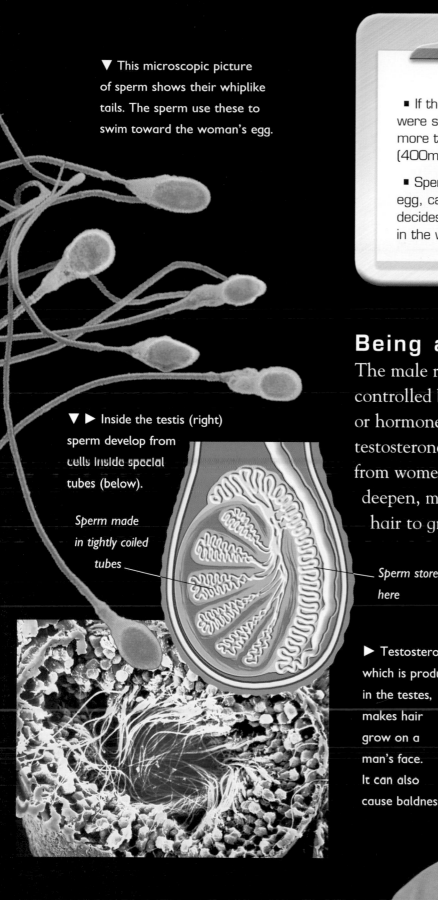

▼ ▶ Inside the testis (right) sperm develop from cells inside special tubes (below).

Sperm made in tightly coiled tubes

Sperm stored here

▶ Testosterone, which is produced in the testes, makes hair grow on a man's face. It can also cause baldness.

The female reproductive system

A woman's body has special organs that allow her to become pregnant and have a baby. These organs form the reproductive system. They include the ovaries, the fallopian tubes, the uterus (or womb), and the vagina.

The ovaries

A woman has two ovaries—each one the size and shape of a large almond. They are full of thousands of cells called eggs, or ova. Each month several eggs mature, but only one is released. The egg travels down one of the woman's fallopian tubes toward the uterus.

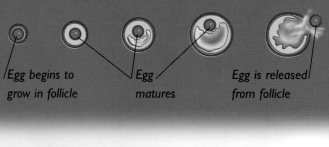

Egg begins to grow in follicle

Egg matures

Egg is released from follicle

Remains of follicle break down if fertilization does not happen

◄ Inside the ovary each egg grows inside a sac called a follicle. When the egg is mature, it will burst out of the follicle. This is called ovulation, and it happens, on average, once every 28 days.

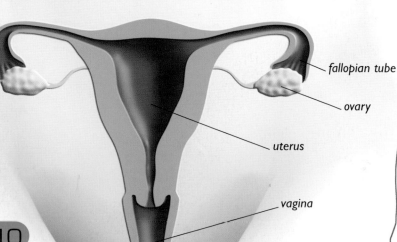

fallopian tube

ovary

uterus

vagina

A woman's reproductive system is found here

▶ Each month eggs start to grow in the ovary. After two weeks one mature egg is released. If this egg is not fertilized, a new monthly cycle begins.

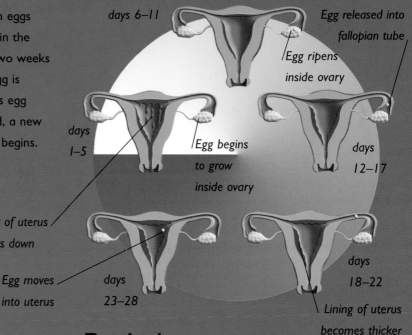

days 6–11

Egg released into fallopian tube

Egg ripens inside ovary

days 1–5

Egg begins to grow inside ovary

days 12–17

Lining of uterus breaks down

Egg moves into uterus

days 23–28

days 18–22

Lining of uterus becomes thicker

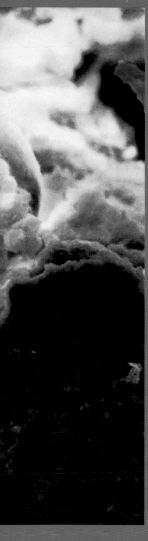

▲ An egg (pink) bursts out of an ovary. It will move down a fallopian tube and may be joined, or fertilized, by a sperm.

▲ Most girls begin to have periods, or to menstruate, between the ages of 11 and 14 years old. Menstruation continues until the age of around 50 years old.

Periods

In most months the woman does not become pregnant. Instead the lining of the uterus breaks down and is shed along with the unfertilized egg through the vagina. This causes bleeding, known as menstruation or a period. Around five days later the lining of the uterus begins to thicken again.

Info lab

- When a baby girl is born, her ovaries contain between one million and two million eggs, or ova.

- A woman will release more than 400 eggs during her lifetime.

- By the age of 50 most women stop ovulating. This is called menopause.

Getting ready

While the egg is maturing in the ovary, the lining of the uterus becomes thick with blood vessels. This prepares the uterus for pregnancy, which takes place if the egg is fertilized by a sperm.

In the beginning

Every human life begins in the same way—when a sperm from a man joins with an egg from a woman. In order to do this, the man puts his penis inside the woman's vagina. Millions of sperm are released that swim toward the egg. If one breaks through the egg's outer layer, fertilization takes place.

The long voyage

In order to reach an egg, sperm must swim up the uterus and into the fallopian tubes—a journey that is several thousand times their own length. Of the millions of sperm that start the journey, only a small fraction will reach the egg, and only one will fertilize it.

Let's divide

When the egg has been fertilized, it continues to travel through the fallopian tube. As it does this, the new cell divides into two, and then four, and so on. Around three days after fertilization a ball of 16 cells arrives in the uterus.

▶ This sperm has broken through the surface of the egg. It will lose its tail and fuse with the nucleus in the center of the egg.

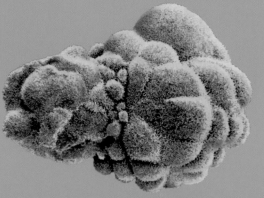

▶ This is a fertilized egg after six days.

Info lab

- It takes several hours for sperm to make the journey to the egg.

- Sperm can survive for several days in the uterus or fallopian tubes.

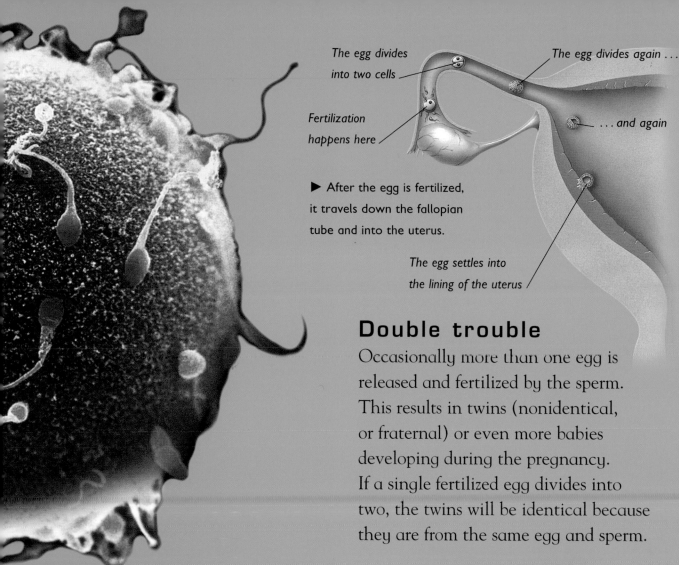

The egg divides into two cells

The egg divides again . . .

Fertilization happens here

. . . and again

▶ After the egg is fertilized, it travels down the fallopian tube and into the uterus.

The egg settles into the lining of the uterus

Double trouble

Occasionally more than one egg is released and fertilized by the sperm. This results in twins (nonidentical, or fraternal) or even more babies developing during the pregnancy. If a single fertilized egg divides into two, the twins will be identical because they are from the same egg and sperm.

▲ Several hundred sperm surround an egg. In order to attract sperm toward it, the egg releases a special chemical signal.

▶ Identical twins are born when a single fertilized egg divides to start two new lives rather than only one.

The journey ends

Six or seven days after fertilization the egg has grown to be around 100 cells. It is now ready to attach itself to the lining of the uterus. This is the beginning of pregnancy. The cells on the inside of the egg will grow into the new baby.

Early pregnancy

During the first three months of pregnancy the tiny baby and its mother both go through dramatic changes. In just a few weeks the ball of cells grows hundreds of times in size. By the fifth week the baby's heart has begun to beat. After twelve weeks the baby has a face, can frown, and move its limbs.

▶ Inside the womb the 12-week-old fetus floats in a sac of fluid. This liquid, called amniotic fluid, cushions the baby.

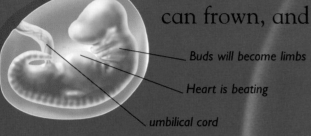

Buds will become limbs

Heart is beating

umbilical cord

▲ At four weeks old the embryo is the size of a pea.

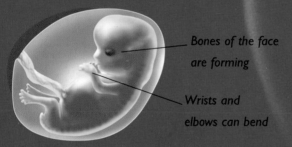

Bones of the face are forming

Wrists and elbows can bend

▲ By eight weeks old the fetus is around the size of a strawberry.

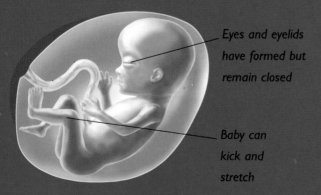

Eyes and eyelids have formed but remain closed

Baby can kick and stretch

▲ Twelve weeks after fertilization the fetus is around the size of a lemon.

Four weeks

One month after fertilization the ball of cells is called an embryo. It has a tail and looks more like a tadpole than a human being! The heart and other organs are forming, but the arms and legs have not developed yet.

Eight weeks

The embryo is now called a fetus. It has a face, with eyes that are closed, along with a mouth and tongue. Fingers and toes have now formed. Inside its body the organs are growing fast.

Twelve weeks

All of the organs, limbs, muscles, and bones are in place. The head is still large compared to the rest of the body, but the fetus now looks like a baby. It is also possible to tell if it is a boy or a girl.

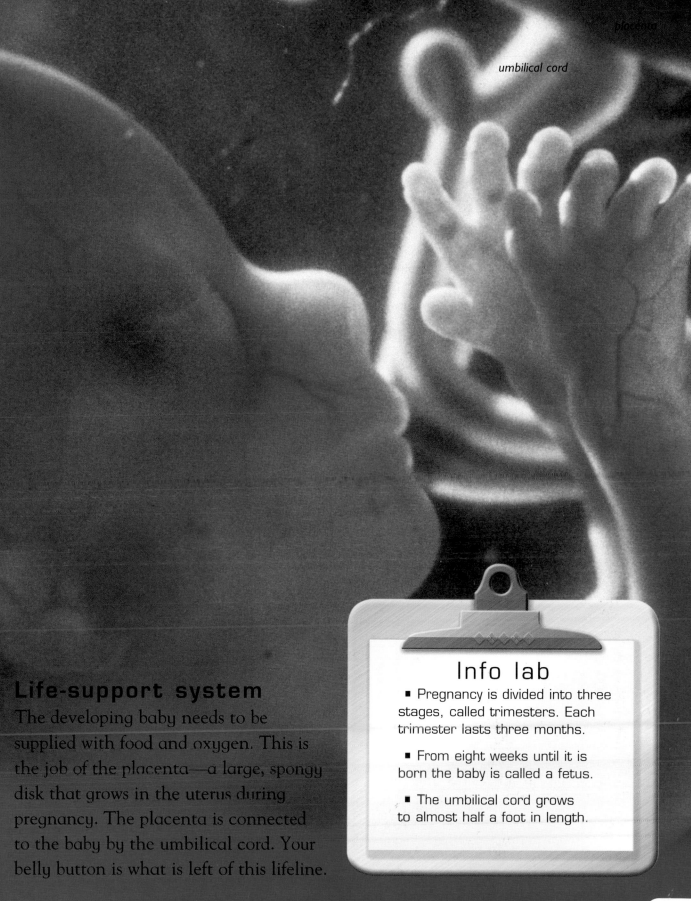

placenta

umbilical cord

Life-support system

The developing baby needs to be supplied with food and oxygen. This is the job of the placenta—a large, spongy disk that grows in the uterus during pregnancy. The placenta is connected to the baby by the umbilical cord. Your belly button is what is left of this lifeline.

Info lab

■ Pregnancy is divided into three stages, called trimesters. Each trimester lasts three months.

■ From eight weeks until it is born the baby is called a fetus.

■ The umbilical cord grows to almost half a foot in length.

Later pregnancy

After three months of pregnancy all the baby's organs, muscles, and bones will have formed. But it is still very small and would not be able to survive in the outside world. During the next six months the baby must grow 100 times in weight before it is ready to be born.

▲ Between 16 and 22 weeks of pregnancy the mother may start to feel the baby moving inside her.

Growing fetus

Between 22 to 24 weeks the baby measures around 8 in. (20cm) in length. The fingers have nails, as well as ridges that will become fingerprints. A layer of fine hair, called lanugo, covers the baby's skin. This hair disappears before birth.

▶ Between 38 and 40 weeks the baby is ready to be born. It will journey through the vagina and out into the world.

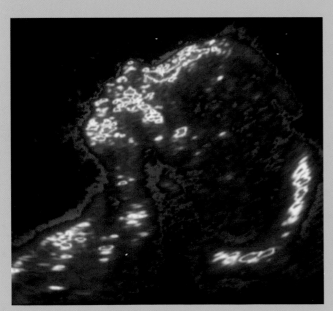

Amniotic fluid surrounds the baby

▲ This ultrasound (sonogram) shows the head and upper body of a 22-week-old fetus. The baby may move when it hears its mother's voice or when her abdomen is touched.

Watching the baby

Although the fetus is hidden away in the womb, a special test—called an ultrasound or sonogram—allows doctors to see inside the uterus. This test is used to measure the baby, to watch its heart beating, to check for twins, and to detect any problems.

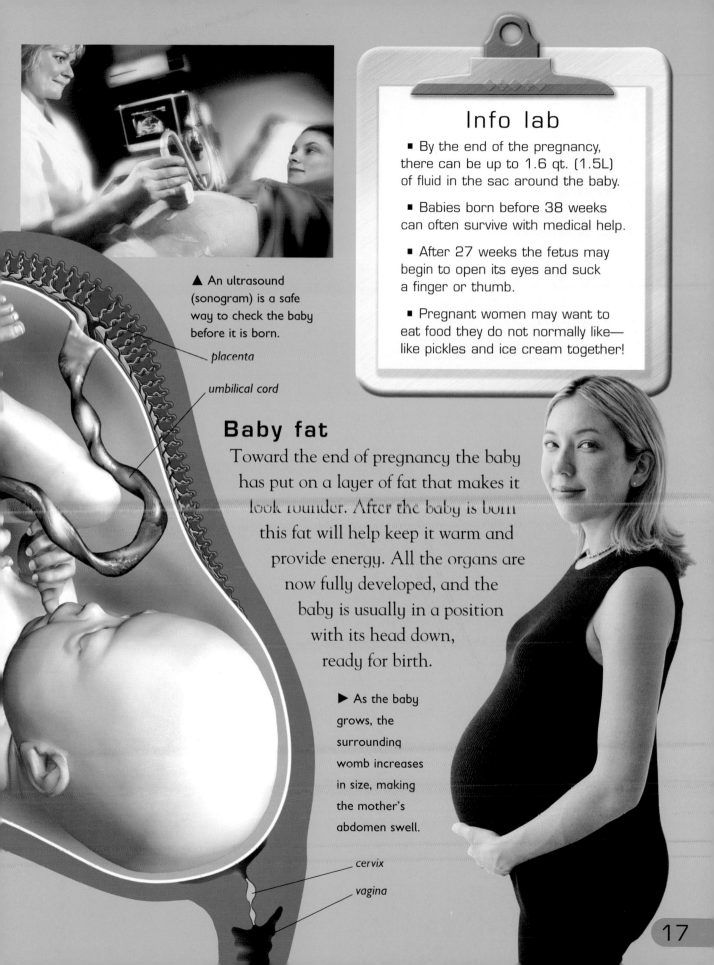

▲ An ultrasound (sonogram) is a safe way to check the baby before it is born.

placenta

umbilical cord

Baby fat

Toward the end of pregnancy the baby has put on a layer of fat that makes it look rounder. After the baby is born this fat will help keep it warm and provide energy. All the organs are now fully developed, and the baby is usually in a position with its head down, ready for birth.

▶ As the baby grows, the surrounding womb increases in size, making the mother's abdomen swell.

cervix

vagina

17

Birth

Around nine months after the egg is fertilized the baby is ready to be born. The mother will feel powerful movements, called contractions, in her uterus. This is one of the signs that labor has begun. During labor the baby is pushed out into the world.

▲ The first stage of labor involves pushing the baby's head into the mother's vagina, or birth canal.

▲ During the second stage the mother's contractions push the baby out of her body.

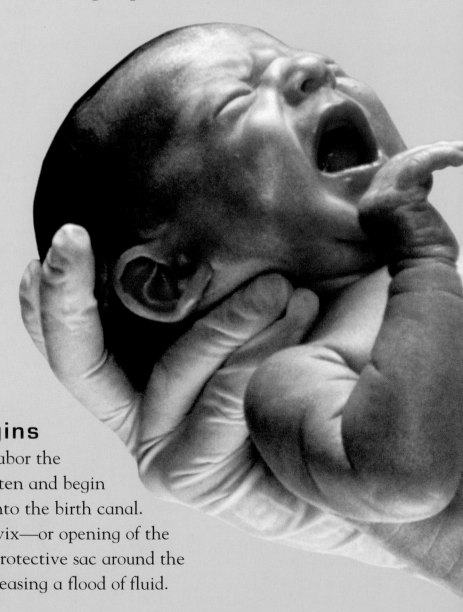

▲ After the baby is born the placenta, with the umbilical cord attached, passes through the birth canal.

The journey begins

During the first stage of labor the muscles of the uterus tighten and begin to squeeze the baby out into the birth canal. At the same time the cervix—or opening of the uterus—gets wider. The protective sac around the baby may break open, releasing a flood of fluid.

Pushing hard

The second stage of labor begins after the cervix has stretched wide enough to allow the baby to move through the birth canal. With each contraction, the mother usually feels a very strong urge to push the baby out farther. Finally the baby is born.

Afterbirth

Once the baby is born, the uterus continues to contract—but much more gently. It still has one more job to do. The placenta—sometimes called the afterbirth—is no longer needed and must also be delivered. This is the third stage of labor.

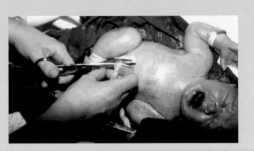

◀ Soon after birth the baby's umbilical cord is cut.

◀ A newborn baby opens its mouth and cries. This fills the baby's lungs with air.

19

Inheritance

Have you ever wondered why you look the way that you do? Genes—the instructions that tell your body how to build itself—have the biggest influence. If you look like your parents or your brother or sister, this is because genes are inherited, or passed on, during reproduction.

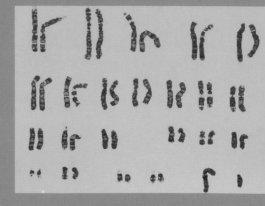

▲ ▼ A cell's nucleus contains 23 pairs of chromosomes. The genes inside each pair control how your body is put together.

▼ You can see similar features across four generations of females from the same family.

cell

nucleus

chromosomes

Info lab

- Half of all your genes are the same as a banana's genes!

- There are around 25,000 pairs of genes inside each cell's nucleus.

▲ An egg fertilized by a sperm carrying an X chromosome will develop into a girl.

Chromosomes

Your body is made up of trillions of tiny units, or cells. Each cell has a control center called a nucleus. This is where your genes are stored. The genes are found in stringlike strands called chromosomes.

Odd one out

There are 23 pairs of chromosomes inside most cells in your body. But egg and sperm cells are different. Instead of pairs of chromosomes, they only have one of each of the 23 chromosomes.

Joining together

During fertilization the set of 23 chromosomes from the egg and the set of 23 chromosomes from the sperm join together. This means that the new baby has 46 chromosomes altogether and inherits a mixture of genes from both parents.

Boys and girls

A pair of chromosomes called the sex chromosomes controls whether a fetus develops as a boy or a girl. Girls have two of the same type of sex chromosome, called X chromosomes. Boys have two different types of sex chromosomes—one X and one Y chromosome. It is the Y chromosome that makes them boys.

▼ If the sperm that joins the egg carries the Y chromosome, the fetus will become a boy.

Why we look different

Walk down the street, and you will see all types of different people—large and small, short and tall, fair and dark. Although we are all built in the same way, there are tiny differences in our genes that help make each one of us unique.

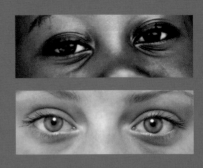

▲ Your genes alone are responsible for the color of your eyes.

More than just your genes

Some features, such as the color of your hair and eyes, are controlled by genes. But others depend both on your genes and what you experience. So while a person may have inherited the genes to be tall, sickness or poor diet may stop him or her from reaching full height.

Body shapes

In colder regions of the world bodies tend to be stocky, and ears and feet are small. This helps prevent heat loss. In very hot climates people are often tall and thin, with larger ears and noses so that heat can escape quickly.

◄ Each one of us looks different, even though we share almost exactly the same genes.

◀ The Masai tribespeople of Kenya, in Africa, have dark skin to protect them from the fierce sun. Long limbs allow heat to escape and keep them cool.

▶ The Inuit people of northern Canada have stocky bodies. This helps them stay warm. But they still need fur clothing to survive the cold.

You are what you eat

Exercise and a healthy diet can make a difference in your appearance. They help you build muscles and prevent you from becoming overweight. For some people lack of exercise and eating junk food have the opposite effect.

▲ Swimmers develop broad shoulders and strong arms in order to pull themselves through the water.

Life as a baby

▲ A newborn baby can grasp an adult's finger very tightly. This is called a reflex.

A newborn baby certainly knows how to cry! At birth babies are helpless and completely dependent on others. Crying is the only way to get attention. But by the end of the first year, the infant may be playing simple games, learning a few words, and taking his or her first steps.

On the move

At first the baby's muscles are weak, and it cannot lift its head. Slowly the baby learns how to roll over and sit up without falling over. By around nine months the baby can crawl and stand up straight without help.

▼ A strong bond between baby and parents is very important. Lots of eye contact and attention will help the baby develop into a confident and happy child.

Magic milk

Babies are able to feed from their mother's breast or a bottle as soon as they are born. In the first few months breast milk contains all the ingredients a baby needs in order to grow, as well as a few extra ones to help fight infections.

First words

At first babies learn by copying their parents. After a few months, a baby can smile. By nine months the baby can babble and shout. By one year a baby can say a few simple words.

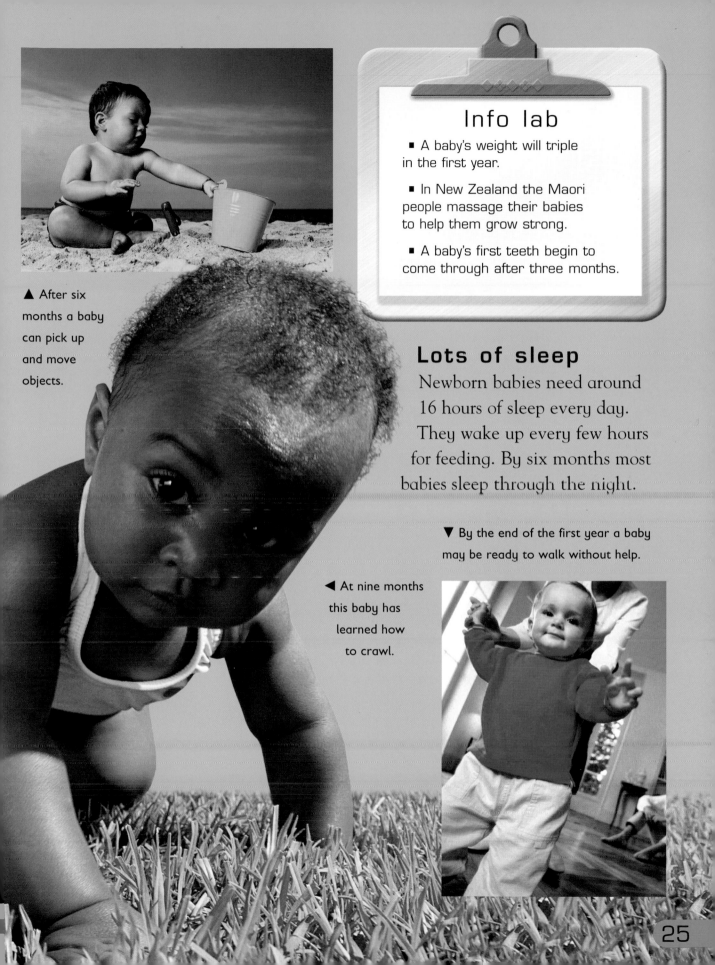

▲ After six months a baby can pick up and move objects.

Lots of sleep

Newborn babies need around 16 hours of sleep every day. They wake up every few hours for feeding. By six months most babies sleep through the night.

▼ By the end of the first year a baby may be ready to walk without help.

◄ At nine months this baby has learned how to crawl.

Childhood

Infancy comes to an end after the first year of a person's life. During the next few years children become more confident in their movements. They learn how to count and later how to read and write. During childhood the body continues to grow.

Growth

Different parts of the body grow at different speeds during childhood. In the first year the head appears very large. From the age of two, the body, including the arms and legs, becomes longer. At this age there is a thick layer of fat under the skin. This creates a baby-faced look. But from around five years old the face loses this layer of fat, and the features become much sharper.

Fast learners

By the age of two children are putting together words to make simple sentences. Two years later they can have a conversation with another person and begin to use words to express their feelings. Reading and writing start by the age of five years old.

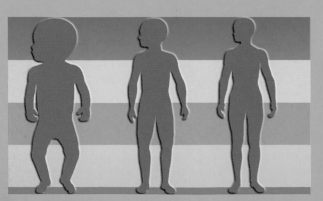

◀ At birth a baby's head is one fourth the size of its body. The head reaches its full adult size— one seventh the length of the body— at 15 years old.

▲ This X-ray image shows an adult tooth (green) ready to push out a baby tooth just above it. Adult teeth replace baby teeth between the ages of six and 14 years old.

Child's play

Playing with other children is a fun and important part of a child's life. Through play children learn to communicate with others, to practice new skills, and to work as part of a team.

▶ Around the age of four children begin to form friendships. Playing together lets children explore the world in new ways.

◀ Children learn all types of skills as they grow older. Many of these skills will be needed for the rest of their lives.

Info lab

- By the age of two, most children have reached half their adult height.

- By the age of five, a child can draw and describe pictures.

Child to adult

Between the ages of 10 and 14 boys and girls notice major changes happening to their bodies. Except for when we are babies, this time—called puberty—is when we grow the most rapidly. Our bodies develop adult features, and our reproductive systems begin to work. Feelings and the way we behave also change as childhood is left behind.

▲ Teenage girls and boys are often very aware of their bodies and how they look.

▶ The time of change when teens become more independent and mature is called adolescence.

Becoming a woman

From the age of 10 or 11 years old a girl's shape begins to change. As well as growing taller, her breasts develop, and her hips become wider. Inside her body the ovaries and uterus are also growing. By the age of 12 or 13, she has her first menstrual period.

▼ During puberty the proportions of the body change. Girls become curvier, while boys become broader and more muscular.

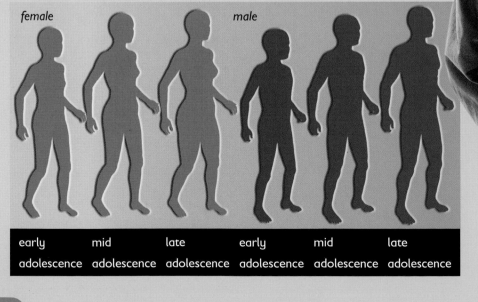

female   male

| early adolescence | mid adolescence | late adolescence | early adolescence | mid adolescence | late adolescence |

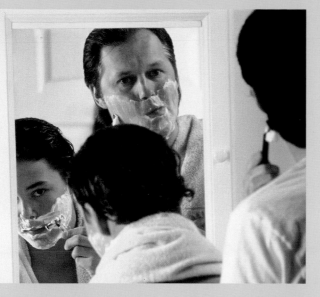

▲ Shaving is one new skill teenage boys need to learn. Puberty makes hair on the face grow thicker and faster.

Boy to man

Puberty arrives a little later for a boy than a girl—usually between the ages of 12 and 14. The boy's height increases rapidly, and over the next few years his body becomes broader and more muscular. His voice deepens, and hair appears on his face.

New challenges

Adolescence is an exciting and challenging time. Teenagers may start a special relationship with a boyfriend or a girlfriend. Life often appears to become more complicated as teenagers face important decisions and experience new feelings and mood changes.

Rites of passage

In every country around the world, people celebrate important events in a person's life. The passage from one stage of life to another is often marked by a ceremony. These ceremonies are known as rites of passage.

▲ A Native American girl is blessed with a sprinkling of pollen. From now on she will no longer be thought of as a child.

First rites

The birth of a child is celebrated in every culture. In many religions prayers are often made to welcome the child into the world, and the baby is given a name.

▶ These aboriginal boys in Australia have had their bodies decorated in a ceremony that prepares them for manhood. They are also taught traditional songs and dances.

◀ This Sami baby from Norway has just been given a first name in a special ceremony.

Endurance test

In New Guinea when girls of the Arapesh tribe reach puberty, they have to remain in huts for six days. When they emerge, they are treated as adults. Similar tests marking the end of childhood are found in traditional cultures around the world

► A young Hindu woman is blessed at her wedding. Marriage is one of the most important rites of passage in many cultures.

Coming of age

Most countries have laws that set a minimum age when you can drive a car, get married, or vote. In Japan young people celebrate this at the age of 20 in a festival called the Coming of Age Day.

The final chapter

When someone dies, a funeral takes place. Some cultures believe that death is a journey, and the funeral allows the person's spirit to move on to the next world. In China paper models of cars or airplanes are sometimes made to help the dead person on this journey.

Adulthood

Once you become an adult, you stop growing. But the body must continue to take care of itself, repairing damage and replacing cells that die or are lost. As the years pass, these repairs do not work as well. Some cells die and cannot be replaced. This leads to changes in the body that we call aging.

▲ During their 20s and 30s men and women often form long-term relationships and decide to have children.

Being an adult

When you are an adult, you are free to decide how you want to live your life. You can choose a career, travel the world, or start your own family. Adulthood also brings important responsibilities such as raising children or caring for elderly relatives.

▲ Wrinkles and lines develop because the skin gets thinner and less stretchy as a person grows older.

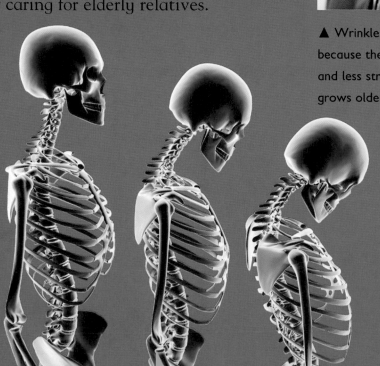

◄ In later years the bones can weaken and even collapse. This causes the spine to curve, and we can become shorter, as seen here from left to right.

◀ After the age of 40 many people need to wear glasses for reading.

▼ Although people often become less physically fit as they get older, many people continue to lead very active lives.

Info lab

- After the age of 25 a person's brain and kidneys begin to shrink slightly.

- By the age of 30 people start losing the ability to hear very high-pitched sounds.

- By the age of 50 half the hairs on the head turn gray.

Signs of aging

As people get older their skin becomes wrinkled, and their hearing becomes less sensitive. But the ability to solve problems and make difficult decisions can improve with age.

Eyesight

Many adults find that they need to start wearing glasses. The lens in the eye becomes larger with age and less able to change its shape. This makes it more difficult to focus on nearby objects, such as a book, which will appear blurry.

Staying healthy

▲ Skiing is just one of many sports that can make your body strong and flexible.

▼ Playing outside is a great way of staying fit. And there are no age limits!

Take care of your body! If you stay physically fit and healthy, you are less likely to get sick. And if you do get sick, you will be able to recover quicker. A good, balanced diet and regular exercise will help you stay healthy throughout your life.

Stay active

Don't just sit there—jump into action! Activities like swimming, dancing, or playing soccer make your muscles and bones strong and keep your heart healthy. Exercise can even release chemicals in your brain that make you feel happy.

Food for life

Fruits and vegetables are full of vitamins that your body needs in order to work properly. Foods that are rich in carbohydrates, such as rice or pasta, give you energy. And don't forget beans, fish, meat, and cheese! These contain protein, which builds up your muscles.

▲ For healthy teeth and gums regular visits to the dentist are essential. But remember to brush your teeth after meals to help prevent tooth decay.

Danger zone

Smoking is one of the most harmful things you can do to your body. Every puff of a cigarette contains thousands of chemicals that include many dangerous poisons. These can damage your heart and blood vessels, clog up your lungs, and harm vital organs.

► Smoking is a major health risk and can shorten a person's life.

▲ Fresh fruits and vegetables are full of vitamins and minerals. These foods also contain fiber, which gets your digestive system working properly.

Prevention

Vaccinations might not be much fun, but they can prevent common illnesses such as measles and mumps. Checkups at the dentist and eye doctor are also important if you want to keep your teeth and eyes in good condition.

Glossary

abdomen The central part of the body between the chest and the hips.

adolescence The stage of life during which a child develops into an adult.

carbohydrate A type of nutrient found in food that the body uses as a supply of energy.

cell The smallest unit, or building block, found in any living organism. Every tissue and organ in the body is made from a collection of cells.

cervix The opening of the uterus, or womb, through which a baby passes during birth.

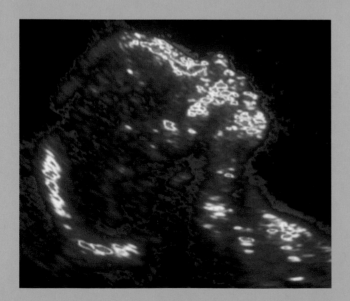

chromosome Tiny, threadlike structures containing genes that are found in every cell of your body.

egg see **ovum**

fertilization The joining together of a female sex cell (egg) and a male sex cell (sperm). A fertilized egg develops into a new baby.

genes The instructions that tell the body how to build and run itself.

hormone A chemical message sent around the body in the blood to tell another part of the body what to do.

labor The last stage of pregnancy, during which the womb contracts to push the baby out.

nucleus The control center of a cell. This is where the chromosomes are found.

nutrients Substances found in food and drinks that the body needs for energy, growth, and repair. Nutrients include protein, carbohydrates, and vitamins.

organ A major part of the body such as the heart or the kidneys. Each organ carries out a specific task.

ovary A small organ in a woman's abdomen that makes and releases eggs, or ova. A woman has two ovaries.

ovulation The release of a female sex cell (an egg, or ovum) from a woman's ovary. This happens once every 28 days.

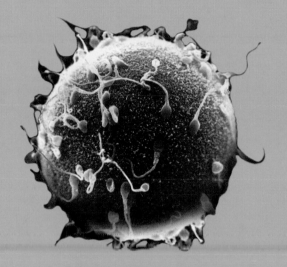

ovum A female sex cell also known as an egg. Eggs, or ova, are made in the ovaries.

pelvis A basin-shaped bone that joins the legs to the lower part of the spine and supports the organs of the abdomen.

placenta A spongy disk that grows inside the womb during pregnancy. It supplies the baby with oxygen and food.

pregnancy The period when a baby is growing inside its mother's uterus, or womb. It usually lasts 40 weeks, beginning with fertilization and ending with birth.

protein A type of nutrient that the body needs for growth and repair.

puberty The stage in life when the reproductive organs start working. It begins between the ages of 10 and 14.

sperm Male sex cells. They are made in the testes.

testes A pair of small, oval-shaped organs found in a man. The testes make sperm and hang outside the body in a sac of skin called the scrotum.

umbilical cord A thick cord that contains blood vessels. It connects the fetus, or developing baby, to the placenta.

uterus A hollow organ found in a woman's abdomen. This is where a fetus grows during pregnancy.

vagina A tube from a woman's womb to the outside of her body, through which a baby is born.

vitamins Chemicals contained in foods. The body needs tiny amounts of vitamins in order to work properly.

womb see **uterus**

Index

Web sites

Keep a count of the number of people
in the world as the population
increases every second:
www.opr.princeton.edu/popclock

See how an unborn baby develops
as it grows in the womb:
www.nlm.nih.gov/medlineplus/ency/
article/002398.htm

A good general introduction
to cells, genes, and DNA:
www.ology.amnh.org/genetics/
index.html

The Kidshealth web site has lots
of information on growing up:
www.kidshealth.org/kid/grow

See how the body changes during
puberty at BBC TV's web site:
www.bbc.co.uk/science/humanbody/
body/interactives/lifecycle/teenagers

Find cartoons, quizzes, and
lots of fun facts to explain
growth, development, aging,
and dozens of other topics
at the BrainPop web site:
www.brainpop.com/health

Learn about the food you need
to stay healthy and strong:
www.nutritionexplorations.org/
kids/main.asp

Acknowledgments

The publisher would like to thank the following for permission
to reproduce their material. Every care has been taken to trace
copyright holders. However, if there have been unintentional
omissions or failure to trace copyright holders, we apologize and will,
if informed, endeavor to make corrections in any future edition.

Key: b = bottom, c = center, l = left, r = right, t = top

Cover tl Science Photo Library (SPL); tc Corbis; bl Getty Imagebank;
br Getty Taxi; page 1 Getty Imagebank; 2–3 SPL; 4 Getty Photographer's
Choice; 6t SPL; 6b Corbis; 7t Getty Imagebank; 7c Corbis; 7b Corbis;
8–9 SPL; 9bl SPL; 9br Corbis; 10–11 SPL; 11c Getty Stone; 12–13 SPL;
14–15 SPL; 16t Getty Stone; 16b SPL; 17t SPL; 17b Corbis; 18–19 Getty
Imagebank; 19cr Imaging Body; 20 SPL; 21t Getty Photographer's Choice;
21b Getty Photodisc; 22tr Corbis; 22cr SPL; 22b Getty Imagebank;
23 Getty Stone; 24tl Getty Stone; 24bl Getty Imagebank; 24–25 Getty
Taxi; 25tl Getty Taxi; 25br Getty Stone; 26tr Getty Imagebank; 26tcr
Getty Imagebank; 26bcr Getty Taxi; 26br Getty Imagebank; 27tl SPL;
27r Getty Stone; 28tl Corbis, 28–29 Getty Taxi; 29tl Getty Stone; 30tl
Still Pictures; 30bl Alamy; 30–31 Alamy; 31tr Getty Stone; 32tl Getty
Stone; 32cr Getty Taxi; 32bl SPL; 32–33 Getty/Taxi; 33tl Getty Taxi;
34tl Corbis; 34–35b Corbis; 35tl Getty Stone; 35cl Alamy; 36 SPL; 37l SPL;
37br Corbis; poster tl Getty Stone; b Getty Taxi; c Getty Stone; tr SPL